THE COURAGEOUS SIX TRIPLE EIGHT

The All-Black Female Battalion of WORLD WAR II

by Dr. Artika R. Tyner

illustrated by Cynthia Paul

Consultant:
Dr. Matthew F. Delmont
Sherman Fairchild Distinguished Professor of History
Dartmouth College

CAPSTONE PRESS
a capstone imprint

Published by Capstone Press, an imprint of Capstone
1710 Roe Crest Drive, North Mankato, Minnesota 56003
capstonepub.com

Library of Congress Cataloging-in-Publication Data
Names: Tyner, Artika R., author. I Paul, Cynthia, illustrator. I Delmont, Matthew F., consultant.
Title: The courageous Six Triple Eight : the all-black female battalion of World War II / by
Artika R. Tyner ; illustrated by Cynthia Paul ; consultant, Dr. Matthew F. Delmont. Other
titles: All-black female battalion of World War II
Description: North Mankato, Minnesota : Capstone Press, [2023] I Series: Women warriors
of World War II I Includes bibliographical references. I Audience: Ages 8–11 I Audience:
Grades 4–6 I Summary: "When the United States entered World War II, it had to face its
own contradictions at home. Opportunities opened up for Black people and women in support
of the war effort. But ideas about race and gender didn't change as swiftly. Read the story
of the first all-Black battalion in the Women's Army Corps—the Six Triple Eight—and its
leader, Major Charity Adams. These women bravely confronted the racism and sexism they
experienced. And they did it while creating a system to make sure millions of letters and
packages got to soldiers fighting in Europe. From the Women Warriors of World War II
graphic novel series, this inspiring story will introduce readers to heroes who were victorious
in more ways than one"—Provided by publisher.
Identifiers: LCCN 2022001288 (print) I LCCN 2022001289 (ebook) I ISBN
9781666334050 (hardcover) I ISBN 9781666334067 (paperback) I ISBN 9781666334074
(pdf) I ISBN 9781666334098 (Kindle edition)
Subjects: LCSH: United States. Army. Women's Army Corps. Central Postal Battalion,
6888th—Juvenile literature. I Earley, Charity Adams, 1918-2002—Juvenile literature. I
African American soldiers—History—20th century—Juvenile literature. I Women soldiers—
History—20th century—Juvenile literature. I Race discrimination—United States—Juvenile
literature. I World War, 1939–1945—Postal service—History—Juvenile literature. I United
States—Armed Forces—Postal service—History—20th century—Juvenile literature. I
CYAC: World War, 1939–1945—Participation, African American—Juvenile literature. I
World War, 1939–1945—Participation, Female—Juvenile literature.
Classification: LCC D769.39 .T96 2023 (print) I LCC D769.39 (ebook) I DDC
940.54/127308996073—dc23/eng/20220126
LC record available at https://lccn.loc.gov/2022001288
LC ebook record available at https://lccn.loc.gov/2022001289

Editorial Credits
Editor: Ericka Smith; Designer: Tracy Davies; Production Specialist: Katy LaVigne

Design Elements: Shutterstock/Here

All internet sites appearing in back matter were available
and accurate when this book was sent to press.

Direct quotations appear in bold italicized text on the following pages:
Pages 14, 20, 21: from June 17, 2020, *New York Times* article, "The Black Female Battalion
That Stood Up to a White Male Army," nytimes.com
Page 19: from Feb. 13, 2017, Department of Defense article, "Sorting the Mail, Blazing a
Trail: African-American Women in World War II," defense.gov
Page 25: from Jan. 22, 2002, *New York Times* article, "Charity Adams Earley, Black Pioneer
in Wacs, Dies at 83," nytimes.com
Page 29: from *One Woman's Army: A Black Officer Remembers the WAC*, by Charity Adams
Earley. College Station: Texas A&M University Press, 1989.

Printed and bound in the USA. 4882

TABLE OF CONTENTS

THE HOPE OF THE AMERICAN DREAM 4

BLACK WOMEN JOIN THE ARMY 8

"NO MAIL, LOW MORALE" 14

FIGHTING OTHER WARS...........................18

SOME WARS CONTINUE...........................24

HOPE FOR THE FUTURE............................28

GLOSSARY 30

READ MORE 31

INTERNET SITES......................................31

ABOUT THE AUTHOR.................................32

ABOUT THE ILLUSTRATOR........................32

THE HOPE OF THE AMERICAN DREAM

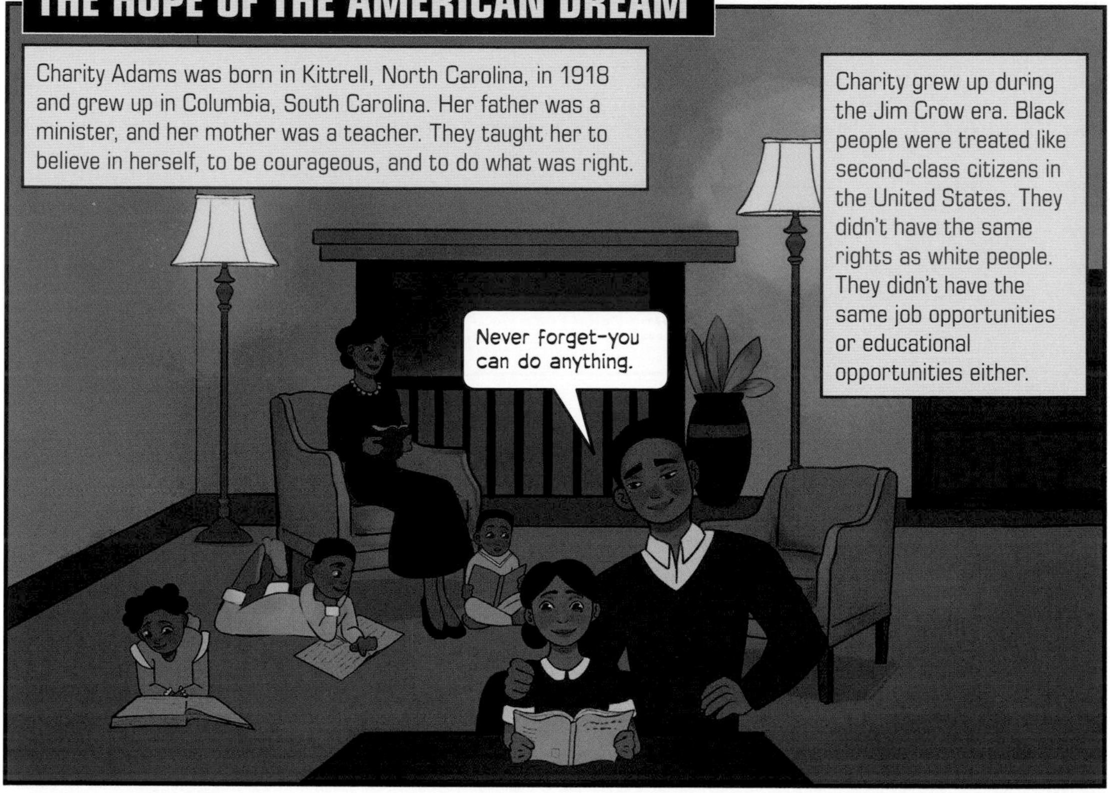
Charity Adams was born in Kittrell, North Carolina, in 1918 and grew up in Columbia, South Carolina. Her father was a minister, and her mother was a teacher. They taught her to believe in herself, to be courageous, and to do what was right.
Charity grew up during the Jim Crow era. Black people were treated like second-class citizens in the United States. They didn't have the same rights as white people. They didn't have the same job opportunities or educational opportunities either.
Never forget—you can do anything.

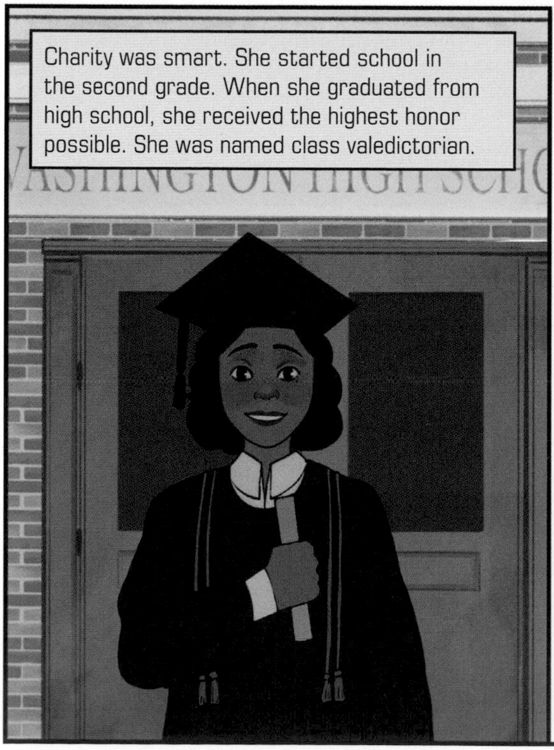
Charity was smart. She started school in the second grade. When she graduated from high school, she received the highest honor possible. She was named class valedictorian.

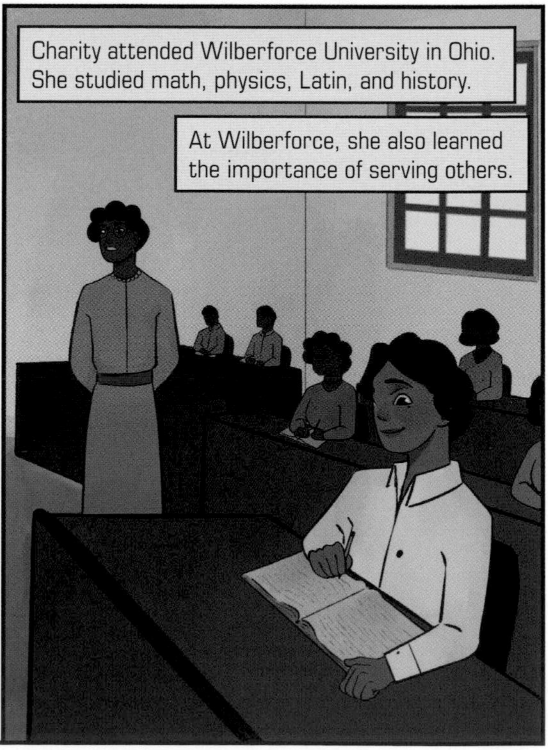
Charity attended Wilberforce University in Ohio. She studied math, physics, Latin, and history.
At Wilberforce, she also learned the importance of serving others.

Charity graduated in 1938. She moved back to Columbia and taught math and science at a segregated junior high school.

One year later, World War II (1939–1945) began when Germany invaded Poland. At first, the United States tried to stay out of the war.

But when the Japanese attacked Pearl Harbor in Hawaii on December 7, 1941, the U.S. quickly joined the war. Soon, the war would change Charity's life too.

After the Pearl Harbor attack, many Americans were eager to serve their country. For Black people, that decision was harder. But some saw it as a way to challenge the second-class citizenship they experienced.

The Double V campaign was created by the *Pittsburgh Courier*. It advocated for equality for Black people. If Black people were helping the country fight for democracy abroad, they should have the rights of full citizenship at home.

This is what it's all about—victory abroad and victory at home.

We are fighting an enemy all the way across the world. But we haven't buried our enemy here at home—this racist Jim Crow system.

Black men joined a segregated army with the hope for better opportunities. Some went overseas to fight. But most worked in service jobs at home.

White folks will have to show us respect as soldiers.

No one will call me "boy" again.

Black women and men also filled important jobs at home outside of the military. Some built ships and airplanes for the war.

BLACK WOMEN JOIN THE ARMY

In May 1941, Congresswoman Edith Nourse Rogers had introduced a bill supporting women joining the army.

Women are prepared to serve in the army. All we need is a fair chance.

But the bill didn't receive much support.

After the attack on Pearl Harbor, many men left for the war overseas, leaving a lot of military roles at home unfilled.

It was time to reconsider the role of women in the army.

EXAMS

SCHOOL NEWS

I WANT YOU FOR U.S. ARMY

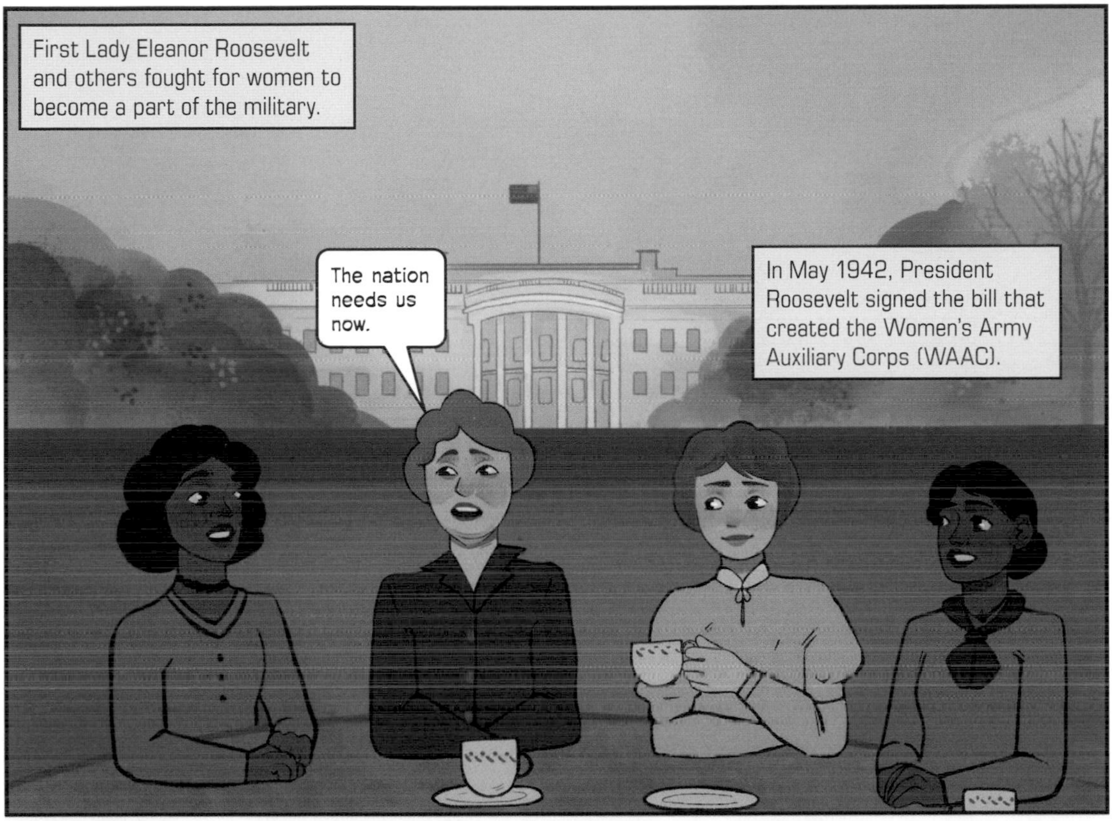
First Lady Eleanor Roosevelt and others fought for women to become a part of the military.
The nation needs us now.
In May 1942, President Roosevelt signed the bill that created the Women's Army Auxiliary Corps (WAAC).

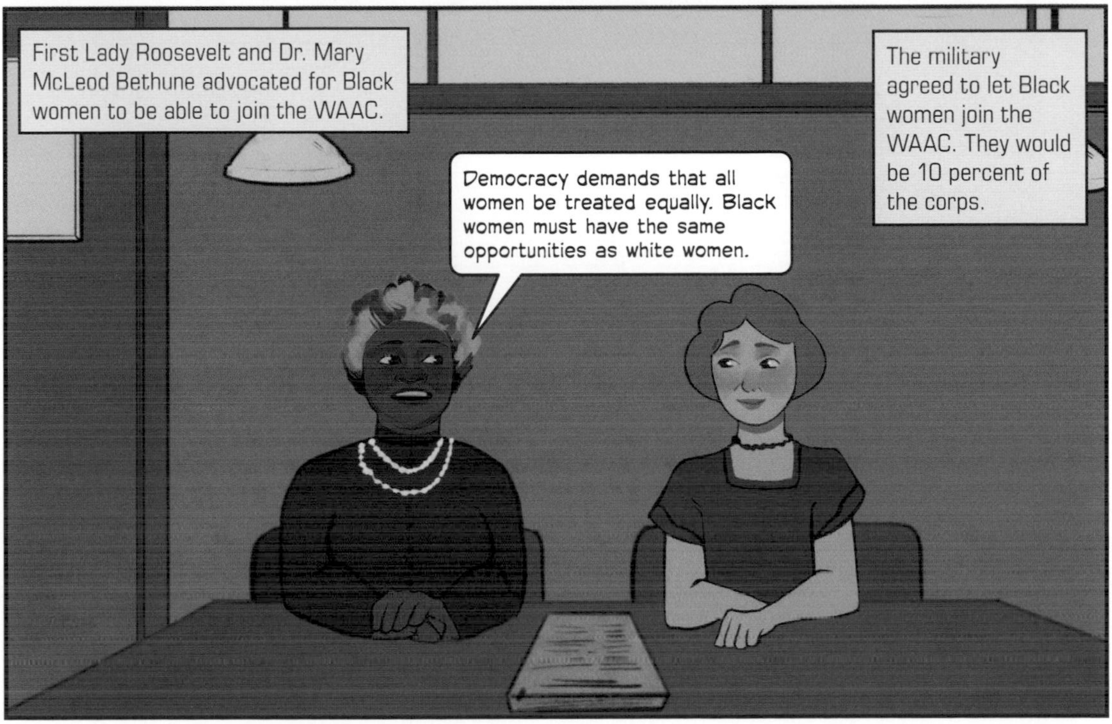
First Lady Roosevelt and Dr. Mary McLeod Bethune advocated for Black women to be able to join the WAAC.
Democracy demands that all women be treated equally. Black women must have the same opportunities as white women.
The military agreed to let Black women join the WAAC. They would be 10 percent of the corps.

Dr. Bethune wanted the brightest and most talented Black women to participate in officer training.

Charity Adams was exactly the type of woman Dr. Bethune was looking for. She applied for the WAAC in June 1942. She received her acceptance letter while taking summer courses at Ohio State University.

Black women across the nation received their acceptance letters too.

Mother, you won't believe it. I was accepted!

Make us proud—come back with a Medal of Honor.

On July 13, 1942, Adams was sworn into the WAAC. She left for training at Fort Des Moines in Iowa.

Reporters came to document this historic moment—Black and white women training together to join the military.

But Black women could never escape the reality of racism. They had separate living quarters. They couldn't use the swimming pool at the same time as white women. And many weren't able to use their training once they were done. They were left to work in areas like laundry services.

Ms. Jones, Ms. Smith, and Ms. Taylor, please follow us. Colored girls, step aside.

Girls?! I see a group of women.

But Adams worked hard while in training.

You can do anything.

Adams was a natural leader and helped train new soldiers. In a little more than a year, she was promoted.

On July 1, 1943, President Roosevelt established the Women's Army Corps (WAC). This was more than a name change. Women were granted the same military rights as men—and could serve overseas.

But it wouldn't be until November 1944 that the military agreed to send Black WACs overseas.

"NO MAIL, LOW MORALE"

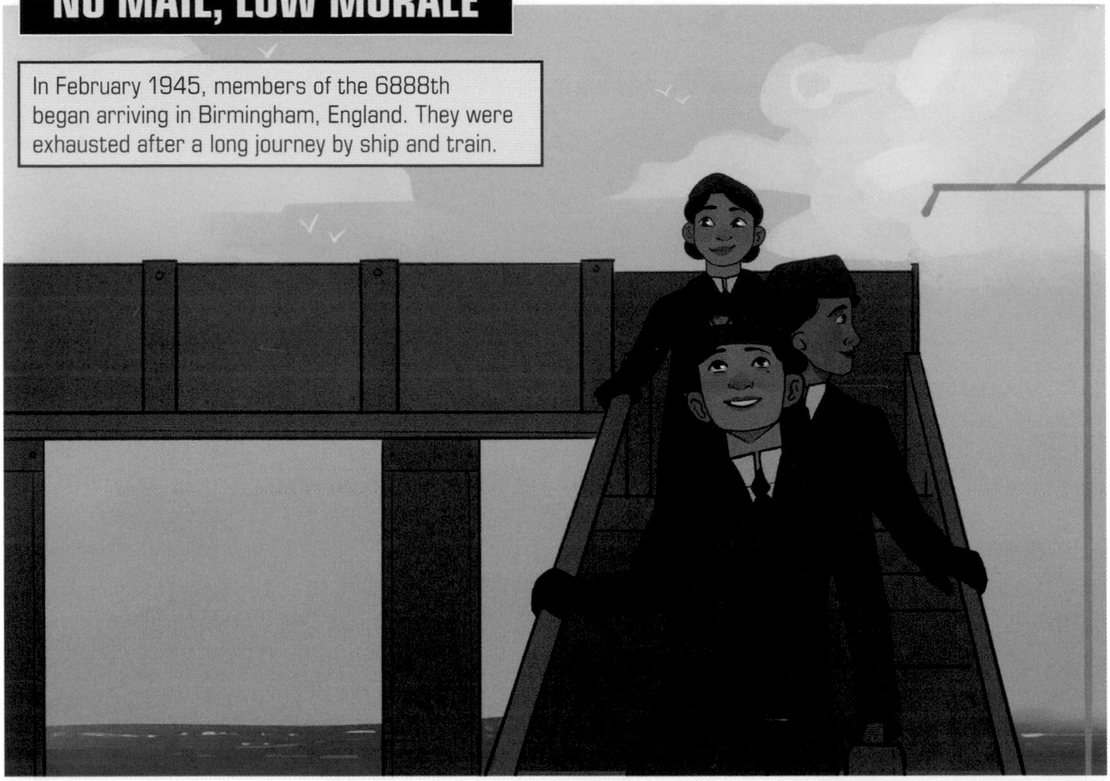
In February 1945, members of the 6888th began arriving in Birmingham, England. They were exhausted after a long journey by ship and train.

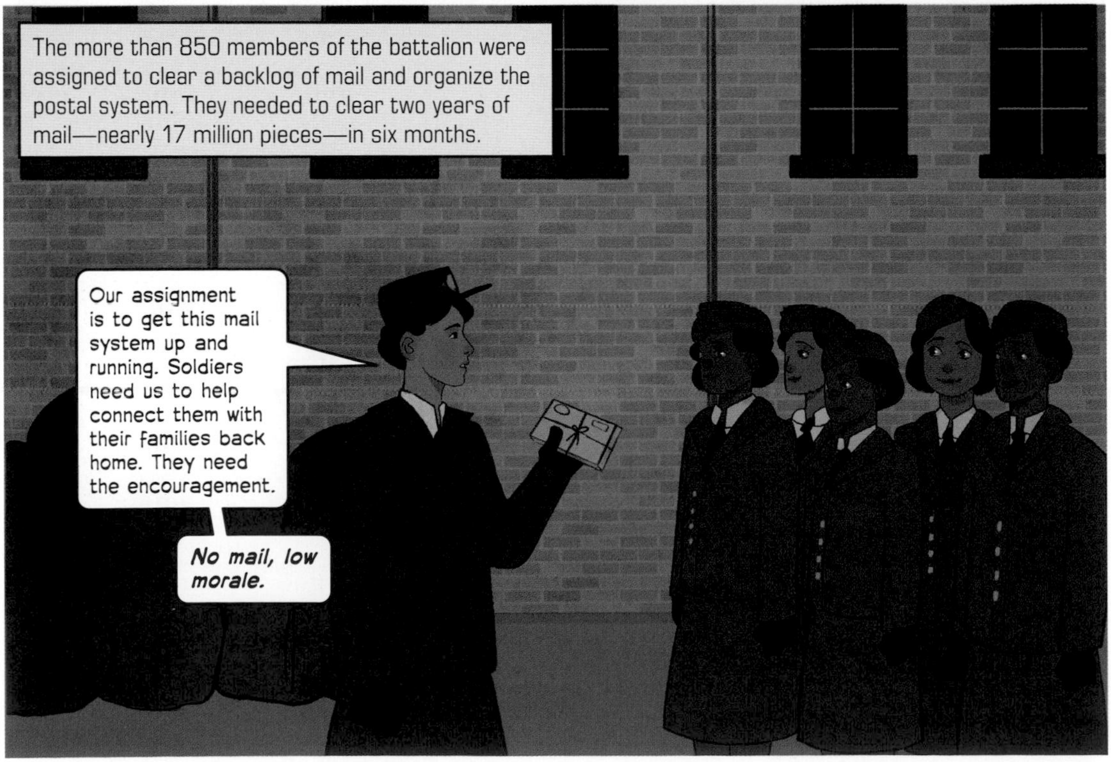
The more than 850 members of the battalion were assigned to clear a backlog of mail and organize the postal system. They needed to clear two years of mail—nearly 17 million pieces—in six months.
Our assignment is to get this mail system up and running. Soldiers need us to help connect them with their families back home. They need the encouragement.
No mail, low morale.

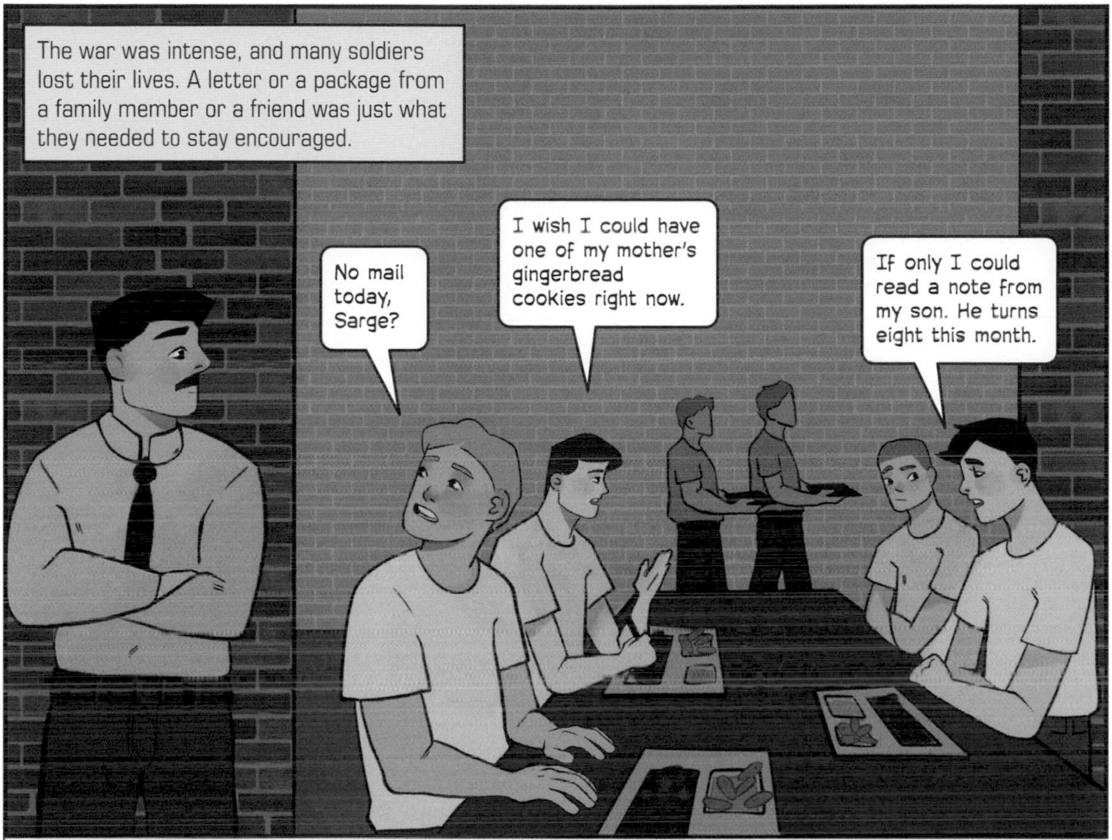
The war was intense, and many soldiers lost their lives. A letter or a package from a family member or a friend was just what they needed to stay encouraged.
No mail today, Sarge?
I wish I could have one of my mother's gingerbread cookies right now.
If only I could read a note from my son. He turns eight this month.

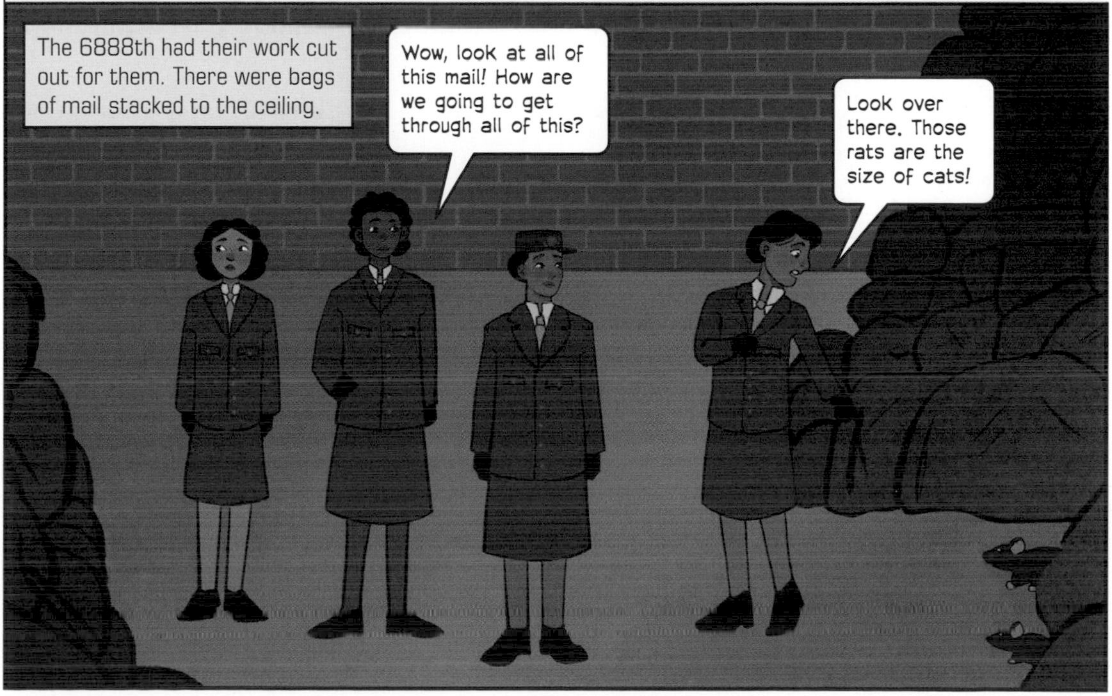
The 6888th had their work cut out for them. There were bags of mail stacked to the ceiling.
Wow, look at all of this mail! How are we going to get through all of this?
Look over there. Those rats are the size of cats!

Adams divided the soldiers into three eight-hour work shifts. And they developed tracking systems to organize the mail. They processed about 65,000 pieces of mail during each shift.

The soldiers also created a system for getting the mail to the right person. They created seven million information cards. Each had a serial number to identify each individual soldier.

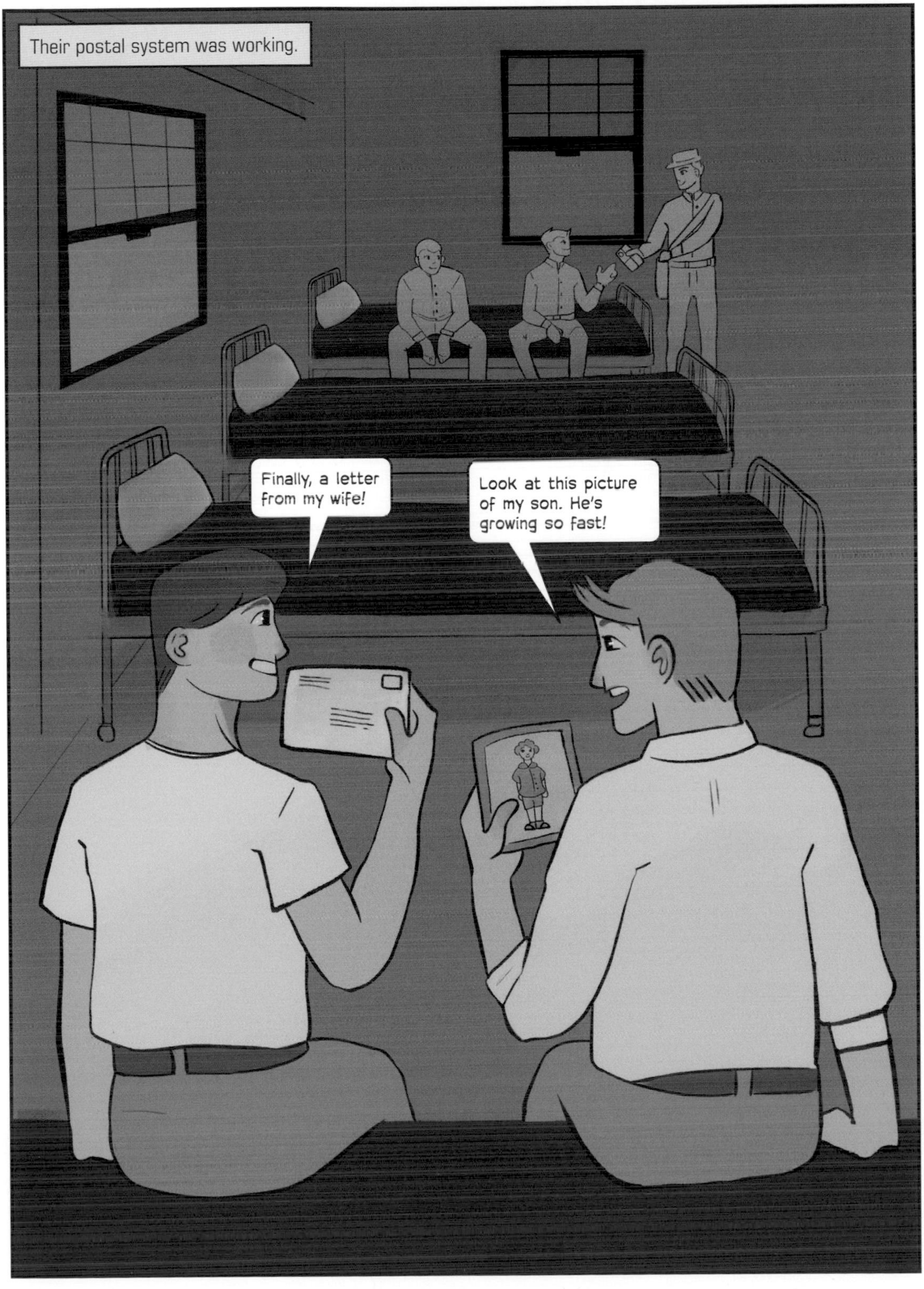
Their postal system was working.
Finally, a letter from my wife!
Look at this picture of my son. He's growing so fast!

FIGHTING OTHER WARS

In their free time, the soldiers enjoyed spending time with their British neighbors. Their experience there was so different from their experience in the United States.

Sometimes the soldiers traveled to London for vacation. When the American Red Cross created a segregated hotel for Black WAC members, Adams was furious. She led a boycott of the hotel.

As long as I am a commanding officer, not one member of that unit will ever spend one night here.

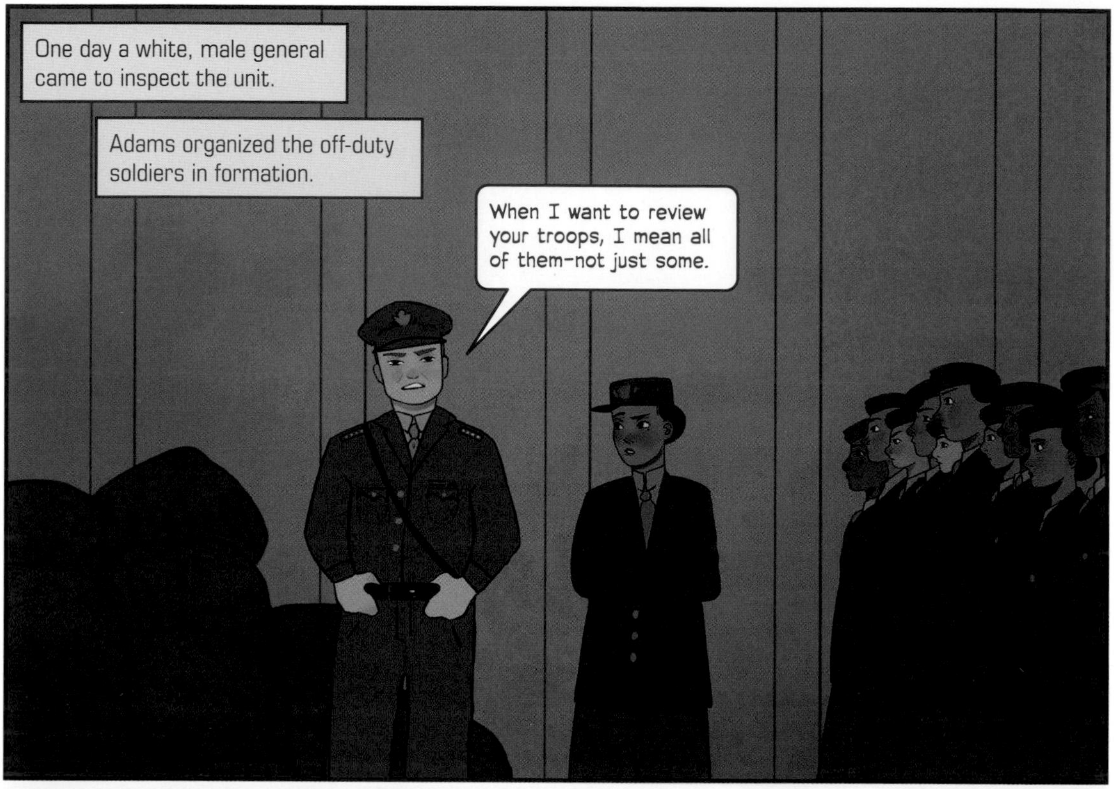
One day a white, male general came to inspect the unit.
Adams organized the off-duty soldiers in formation.
When I want to review your troops, I mean all of them–not just some.

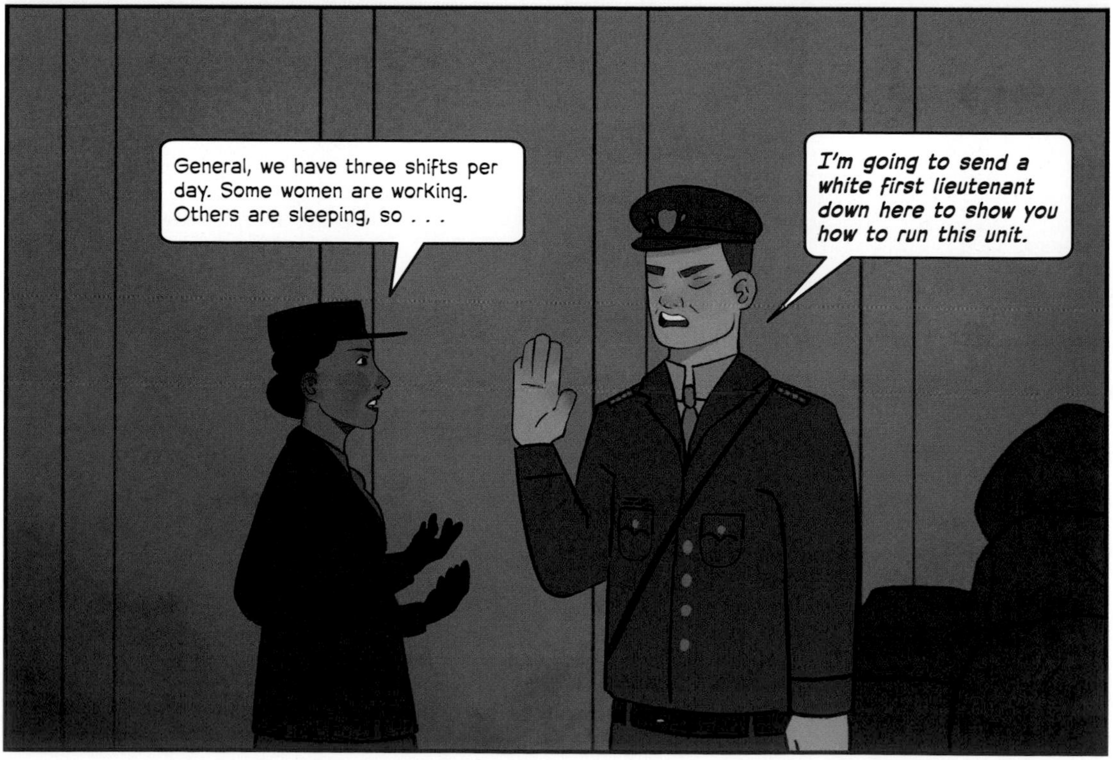
General, we have three shifts per day. Some women are working. Others are sleeping, so . . .
I'm going to send a white first lieutenant down here to show you how to run this unit.

Major Adams had a higher rank than a lieutenant.

Over my dead body, sir.

You will hear from me, Adams.

Adams was punished for protecting her troops. The general filed court-martial charges against her.

But Major Adams prepared her own complaint about the general's racist actions during his visit. He later dropped his charges.

The 6888th persevered in the face of racism and sexism. They worked seven days a week—until they could finally see the floor.

Excellent work, soldiers!

The soldiers were supposed to sort all of the mail within six months—they finished the job in just three. In May 1945, they were sent to Rouen, France, to clear another backlog.

Germany had just surrendered. Fighting in Europe was over.

Let's show them we can accomplish any mission set before us.

Japan officially surrendered in September 1945. World War II was over.

Some members of the 6888th returned home. But those who remained completed a final assignment in Paris, France.

In February 1946, the last soldiers returned to the United States.

We have learned an important lesson about success. It will only come if we all succeed together.

SOME WARS CONTINUE

When the 6888th arrived at Fort Dix, New Jersey, there was no celebration. They were given their discharge papers and sent back to their hometowns.

We worked hard to complete our assignments, and we get no recognition. Where are the parades that the white soldiers received?

After all this, we're still fighting for equality and respect.

The 6888th had returned to the same racist nation they'd left. So they got back to work fighting their second war. They began to organize voter registration drives, raise money for Black college students, and support Black-owned businesses.

WHITE

COLORED

We've got to keep fighting. What should we do?

We know there is power in the ballot box. Are your brother and sister registered to vote?

While many Black veterans were denied G.I. Bill benefits, members of the 6888th were able to use them to continue their education.

Elizabeth Barker Johnson went to Winston-Salem Teachers College. She went on to teach for 30 years.

In December 1945, Adams was promoted to Lieutenant Colonel—the highest possible rank for a soldier in the WAC. Not long after, she ended her military service in March 1946. She wanted to return to graduate school.

She was recognized for her work by Dr. Bethune and the National Council of Negro Women.

You served our country with great courage and unwavering determination.

After the war ended, Adams and the 6888th would get together for reunions and other special occasions. They had become a family.

Lieutenant Colonel Charity Adams Earley died on January 13, 2002, in Dayton, Ohio. She was 83 years old.

"When I talk to students, they say, 'How did it feel to know you were making history?' But you don't know you're making history when it's happening. I just wanted to do my job."
—Charity Adams Earley

In 2009—more than 60 years after World War II ended—the U.S. Army finally recognized the remarkable work of the 6888th Central Postal Directory Battalion.

U.S. ARMY CELEBRATES BLACK WACs OF WORLD WAR II

In March 2009, Mary Ragland and Alyce Dixon of the 6888th were honored at the Women's History Month event at Arlington National Cemetery. They met First Lady Michelle Obama.

In 2018, a monument dedicated to the 6888th was placed at the Buffalo Soldier Monument Park in Fort Leavenworth, Kansas.

THE 6888TH

THE 6888TH

We did change things.

We sure did. We fought so many wars all at once. We showed them that an all-Black, female battalion was unstoppable.

HOPE FOR THE FUTURE

The 6888th Central Postal Directory Battalion created a legacy worthy of honor. They demonstrated courage, patriotism, and leadership.

They helped pave the way for future generations of Black women in the military.

"I have opened a few doors, broken a few barriers, and, I hope, smoothed the way to some degree for the next generation."

—Charity Adams Earley

Colonel Margaret E. Bailey
In 1970, Margaret E. Bailey became the first Black woman to become a colonel in the U.S. Army.

Major General Marcelite Harris
In 1995, Marcelite Harris was the first Black woman to become a major general in the U.S. Air Force.

Admiral Michelle Howard
In 1999, Michelle Howard became the first Black woman to captain a ship in the U.S. Navy. In 2014, she was the first woman to become a four-star admiral in the U.S. Navy.

Lieutenant General Nadja Y. West
In 2015, Nadja Y. West became the first Black surgeon general of the U.S. Army.

GLOSSARY

advocate (AD-vuh-kayt)—to support an idea or plan

backlog (BAK-log)—a large of amount of work that has built up over time

boycott (BOY-kot)—to refuse to take part in something as a way of protesting something unfair

court-martial (KORT-MAR-shuhl)—a trial for members of the military accused of breaking rules or committing a crime

discharge (DIS-chahrj)—a release from a job or organization

G.I. Bill (JEE EYE BIL)—legislation providing financial aid to military veterans for attending college and buying homes

inspect (in-SPEKT)—to look at something carefully

Jim Crow (JIM KROH)—discrimination against Black people in laws and practices

Medal of Honor (MED-uhl UV ON-ur)—the United States' highest award for bravery in combat

persevere (pur-suh-VEER)—to continually try or commit to a certain action or belief

promote (pruh-MOTE)—to give a higher rank in the military

rank (RANGK)—a position within the military

segregate (SEG-ruh-gate)—to keep people of different races apart in schools and other public places

serial number (SIHR-ee-uhl NUHM-ber)—a number that identified a soldier in the military during World War II

valedictorian (val-i-dik-TOHR-ee-uhn)—the student with the highest academic achievement in a graduating class; they usually make a speech during a graduation ceremony

READ MORE

Biskup, Agnieszka. *Angels of Bataan and Corregidor: The Heroic Nurses of World War II*. North Mankato, MN: Capstone, 2023.

Conkling, Winifred. *Heroism Begins with Her: Inspiring Stories of Bold, Brave, and Gutsy Women in the U.S. Military*. New York: Harper, 2019.

Simons, Lisa M. Bolt. *The U.S. WASP: Trailblazing Women Pilots of World War II*. North Mankato, MN: Capstone, 2018.

INTERNET SITES

The National World War II Museum: The SixTripleEight: No Mail, Low Morale
nationalww2museum.org/war/articles/the-sixtripleeight 6888th-battalion

U.S. Army: Creation of the Women's Army Corps
army.mil/women/history/wac.html

Women of the 6888th Central Postal Directory Battalion
womenofthe6888th.org

ABOUT THE AUTHOR

Dr. Artika R. Tyner is a passionate educator, an award-winning author, a civil rights attorney, a sought-after speaker, and an advocate for justice. She lives in Saint Paul, Minnesota, and is the founder of the Planting People Growing Justice Leadership Institute.

ABOUT THE ILLUSTRATOR

Cynthia Paul grew up in Knoxville, Tennessee, and has since moved up and down the East Coast. After a long career of doodling in the margins of her homework, she decided to jump into children's illustration and has loved it ever since. In her free time, she enjoys writing, learning about history, traveling, and trying her hand at baking.